Bui...ant Books

Synonyms and Antonyms

PARENT-TEACHER COLLECTION

Written by
Vicky Shiotsu

Editor: Gillian Snoddy
Illustrator: Darcy Tom
Cover Illustrator: Rick Grayson
Designer/Production: Alicia Schulte
Art Director: Moonhee Pak
Project Director: Stacey Faulkner

Table of Contents

Introduction

About the
Build-a-Skill Instant Books Series

The *Build-a-Skill Instant Books* series features a variety of reproducible instant books that focus on important reading and math skills covered in the primary classroom. Each instant book is easy to make, and once children become familiar with the basic formats that appear throughout the series, they will be able to make new books with little help. Children will love the unique, manipulative quality of the books and will want to read them over and over again as they gain mastery of basic learning skills!

About Build-a-Skill Instant Books:
Synonyms and Antonyms

This book features commonly used synonyms and antonyms in fun and easy-to-make instant books. Children will make flip books, strip books, mini books, and more! As children read and reread their instant books, they will improve their understanding of synonyms and antonyms and increase their vocabulary. For your reference, the synonyms and antonyms that appear in this book are listed on pages 5 and 6.

Refer to the Table of Contents to help with lesson planning. Choose instant book activities that fit with current curriculum goals in your regular or ELL classroom. Use the instant books to practice skills or introduce new ones. Directions for making the instant books appear on pages 3 and 4. To use as a bookmaking activity as homework, provide copies of the directions along with the book patterns.

Making and Using the Instant Books

Most of the instant books in this resource require only one or two pieces of paper. Copy the pages on white copy paper or card stock, or use colored paper to jazz up and vary the formats. Children will love personalizing their instant books by coloring them, adding construction paper covers, or decorating them with collage materials such as ribbon and stickers. Customize the instant books by adding extra pages or by creating your own synonym and antonym cards using the reproducibles on pages 13 and 18.

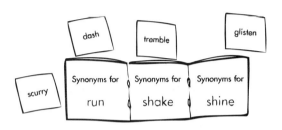

Children can make instant books as an enrichment activity when their regular classwork is done, as a learning center activity during guided reading time, or as a homework assignment. Have children place completed instant books in their classroom book boxes and then read and reread the books independently or with a reading buddy. After children have had many opportunities to read their books in school, send the books home for extra skill-building practice.

Directions for Making the Instant Books

There are six basic formats for the instant books in this guide. The directions appear below and on the next page for quick and easy reference. The directions are written to the child, in case you would like to send the bookmaking activities home as homework. Just copy the directions and attach them to the instant book pages.

> **Hint!** Use the word cards on pages 9–12 with the instant books on pages 7 and 8 to introduce the concepts of synonyms and antonyms. Each card presents a synonym or antonym pair. Use the word cards on pages 16 and 17 with the instant books on pages 14 and 15 to allow children to sort the word cards to create matching pairs. As a rule of thumb, 6–10 cards can be easily stapled onto each instant book.

Flip Books, pages 7, 8

1. Cut out the two flip books, word cards, and blank word pair cards.
2. Staple the word pairs cards to the "I can read" flip book.
3. Staple the blank word pairs cards to the "I can write" flip book.
4. Practice reading and writing pairs of synonyms or antonyms!

Build-a-Skill Instant Books • Synonyms and Antonyms • 2–3 © 2009 Creative Teaching Press

Read-and-Write Book, pages 14, 15

1. Cut out the read-and-write book.
2. Cut out the word cards and sort them into pairs.
3. Staple the cards to the top of the book.
4. Glue the book to construction paper that is the same size.
5. Fold the book in half and decorate the cover.
6. Practice reading the words and writing sentences with them.

Strip Book, pages 19, 20, 24, 26, 28

1. Finish each sentence by writing the correct word.
2. Cut out the strips and put them in order.
3. Staple the book on the left.

Word Wallet, pages 21-22

1. Cut out the wallet. Fold it in half along the solid middle line.
2. Staple where shown. Tape the outer edges. Fold the wallet closed.
3. Cut out the word cards. Sort them into the correct pockets.

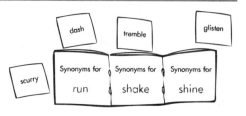

Synonym Mini Book, pages 23, 25

1. Underline the two synonyms on each page.
2. Write the synonyms on the lines.
3. Cut out the pages and put them in order.
4. Staple the book on the left.

Antonym Mini Book, pages 27, 29, 32

1. Underline the two antonyms on each page.
2. Write the antonyms on the lines.
3. Cut out the pages and put them in order.
4. Staple the book on the left.

Accordion-Fold Book, pages 30, 31

1. Finish the book by writing the correct words.
2. Cut along the solid lines to form two strips.
3. Glue one strip onto the other where shown.
4. Fold back and forth along the dashed lines.

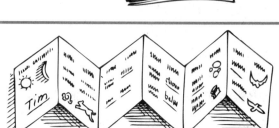

Build-a-Skill Instant Books • Synonyms and Antonyms • 2–3 © 2009 Creative Teaching Press

Synonym Word List

The following synonyms are presented in this book. They are listed in order of first appearance.

afraid	scared	hit	strike	shine	gleam
middle	center	enjoy	like		glisten
depart	leave	road	street		sparkle
display	show	chair	seat		twinkle
easy	simple	bucket	pail	gathering	crowd
hard	difficult	story	tale	yells	shouts
hurry	rush	jump	leap	huge	gigantic
late	tardy	crawl	creep	shining	glistening
pile	heap	toss	throw	grin	smile
pretty	beautiful	pull	tow	chilly	cold
protect	guard	swoop	dive	scorching	hot
repair	fix	steer	drive	showery	rainy
stay	remain	look	peek	breezy	windy
terrible	awful	talk	speak	sunny	bright
vanish	disappear	stumble	trip	cloudy	overcast
fast	swift	hold	grip	foggy	misty
gift	present	run	dash	humid	muggy
help	aid		race	happy	joyful
hide	conceal		scamper	clever	cunning
select	choose		scurry	pretty	lovely
rock	stone	shake	quake	charming	delightful
shine	glow		shiver	foolish	silly
weep	cry		shudder		
bashful	shy		tremble		
unhappy	sad				
angry	mad				

Antonym Word List

The following antonyms are presented in this book. They are listed in order of first appearance.

always	never	thick	thin	wet	dry
bright	dull	lose	win	old	new
build	destroy	push	pull	awake	asleep
clean	dirty	empty	full	outside	inside
attract	repel	short	long	up	down
deep	shallow	weak	strong	fast	slow
friend	enemy	dark	light	day	night
foolish	wise	loose	tight	work	play
joy	sorrow	well	sick	stop	go
many	few	slow	quick	shout	whisper
open	shut	young	old	cry	laugh
poor	rich	outdoors	indoors	give	receive
raw	cooked	messy	neat	slowly	swiftly
sweet	sour	late	early	sets	rises
wide	narrow	love	hate	above	below
back	front	black	white	rough	smooth
boring	exciting	heavy	light	daytime	nighttime
cruel	kind	high	low	smooth	bumpy
lost	found	speedy	slow	plump	slender
sink	float	large	small	moist	dry
tame	wild	short	tall	furry	hairless
come	go	giggle	cry	rounded	pointed

Build-a-Skill Instant Books • Synonyms and Antonyms • 2–3 © 2009 Creative Teaching Press

Synonym Flip Books

Name _____

I can read synonyms.

Name _____

I can write synonyms.

Name _____

I can read antonyms.

Staple word cards here.

Name _____

I can write antonyms.

Staple blank cards here.

Build-a-Skill Instant Books • Synonyms and Antonyms • 2–3 © 2009 Creative Teaching Press

Synonym Pairs Word Cards

Synonyms are words that have the same meaning.

middle	center
display	show
hard	difficult

afraid	scared
depart	leave
easy	simple
hurry	rush

Synonym Pairs Word Cards

late | tardy	pile | heap
pretty | beautiful	protect | guard
repair | fix	stay | remain
terrible | awful	vanish | disappear

Build-a-Skill Instant Books • Synonyms and Antonyms • 2–3 © 2009 Creative Teaching Press

Antonyms are words that have the opposite meaning.

always	bright	clean	deep
	dull	dirty	shallow
never	build	attract	friend
	destroy	repel	enemy

Antonym Pairs Word Cards

foolish	wise
	sorrow
	joy
many	few
	shut
	open
poor	rich
	cooked
	raw
sweet	sour
	narrow
	wide

Build-a-Skill Instant Books • Synonyms and Antonyms • 2–3 © 2009 Creative Teaching Press

Word Pairs Cards

Read-and-Write Synonym Book

Name _____

I can read synonyms.

Staple word cards here.

I can write sentences with synonyms.

_____

_____

_____

_____

_____

Build-a-Skill Instant Books • Synonyms and Antonyms • 2–3 © 2009 Creative Teaching Press

Read-and-Write Antonym Book

Name _____

I can read antonyms.

Staple word cards here.

- -

I can write sentences with antonyms.

_____

_____

_____

_____

_____

Build-a-Skill Instant Books • Synonyms and Antonyms • 2–3 © 2009 Creative Teaching Press

Synonym Word Cards

fast	swift	gift
present	help	aid
hide	conceal	select
choose	rock	stone

Build-a-Skill Instant Books • Synonyms and Antonyms • 2–3 © 2009 Creative Teaching Press

Antonym Word Cards

back	front	boring
exciting	cruel	kind
lost	found	sink
float	tame	wild

Word Cards

Build-a-Skill Instant Books • Synonyms and Antonyms • 2–3 © 2009 Creative Teaching Press

Synonym Strip Book

Synonyms Mean the Same

Synonyms mean the same, like **shine** and **glow**.

Can you pair up synonyms? How many do you know?

1

Another word for **weep** is _____.

Another word for **bashful** is _____.

2

Another word for **unhappy** is _____.

Another word for **angry** is _____.

3

Another word for **hit** is _____.

Another word for **enjoy** is _____.

4

Another word for **road** is _____.

Another word for **chair** is _____.

5

Another word for **bucket** is _____.

Another word for **story** is _____.

6

sad

cry

like

seat

shy

mad

pail

street

tale

strike

Build-a-Skill Instant Books • Synonyms and Antonyms • 2–3 © 2009 Creative Teaching Press

Synonym Strip Book

Synonym Actions

When you **jump** around, you _____.

When you **crawl** along, you _____.

1

When you **toss** a ball, you _____.

When you **pull** a load, you _____.

2

When you **swoop** like a bird, you _____.

When you **steer** a car, you _____.

3

When you **look** in secret, you _____.

When you **talk** to others, you _____.

4

When you walk and then **stumble**, you _____.

When you **hold** something tightly, you _____.

5

Write other pairs of synonym actions!

_____

6

peek

trip

dive

creep

tow

drive

leap

throw

speak

grip

Build-a-Skill Instant Books • Synonyms and Antonyms • 2–3 © 2009 Creative Teaching Press

Synonyms for

run

Synonyms for

shake

Synonyms for

shine

Synonym Wallet

's

Tape here.

Staple here.

Staple here.

Tape here.

Fold here.

Tape here.

Wallet Words: Synonyms

glisten	race	shiver
dash	sparkle	tremble
quake	scurry	gleam
twinkle	shudder	scamper

Build-a-Skill Instant Books • Synonyms and Antonyms • 2–3 © 2009 Creative Teaching Press

Synonym Mini Book

What a Parade!

_____
Name

1

A gathering of people
line the street.
The crowd soon hears
the sound of feet.
Step, step!
Here comes the parade!

_____

_____

2

Someone yells,
"Here comes the band!"
Someone shouts,
"Let's give a hand!"
Clap, clap!
Hurray, hurray!

_____

_____

3

A fancy float
that's huge rolls by.
A gigantic dino
stands up high.
Oh, my!
What a display!

_____

_____

4

A princess with
a shining crown
looks lovely in
a glistening gown.
Ooh, ooh!
She looks great!

_____

_____

5

Clowns grin and play
some silly jokes.
Kids laugh and smile
to see such folks.
Ha, ha!
What a fun-filled day!

_____

_____

6

Synonym Strip Book

All Kinds of Weather

_____
Name

1

A **chilly** day is a _____ day.

A **scorching** day is a _____ day.

2

A **showery** day is a _____ day.

A **breezy** day is a _____ day.

3

A **sunny** day is a _____ day.

A **cloudy** day is an _____ day.

4

A **foggy** day is a _____ day.

A **humid** day is a _____ day.

5

Write a sentence that describes your favorite kind of weather!

_____

6

| overcast |
| windy |
| hot |
| misty |
| bright |
| cold |
| muggy |
| rainy |

Build-a-Skill Instant Books • Synonyms and Antonyms • 2–3 © 2009 Creative Teaching Press

Synonym Mini Book

The Fox and the Crow

_____
Name

1

A crow found a piece of cheese. She was so happy! The joyful bird snatched it up in her beak and flew to a tree.

_____

_____

2

A fox passed by and saw the crow. The clever fox thought of a cunning plan.

_____

_____

3

"How pretty you look," the fox said to the crow. "Your lovely feathers shine in the sun." The crow's heart burst with pride.

_____

_____

4

The fox continued, "I have heard you sing before. You have a charming voice. It would be delightful to hear you sing again."

_____

_____

5

The foolish crow opened her mouth to sing. Out fell the cheese! The silly bird could only watch as the fox gulped down the cheese.

_____

_____

6

Antonym Strip Book

Antonyms Are Opposites

Antonyms are opposites, like **come** and **go**.

Can you pair up antonyms? How many do you know?

1

The opposite of **thick** is _____.

The opposite of **lose** is _____.

2

The opposite of **push** is _____.

The opposite of **empty** is _____.

3

The opposite of **short** is _____.

The opposite of **weak** is _____.

4

The opposite of **dark** is _____.

The opposite of **loose** is _____.

5

The opposite of **well** is _____.

The opposite of **slow** is _____.

6

---

tight

win

long

full

sick

strong

quick

thin

pull

light

Build-a-Skill Instant Books • Synonyms and Antonyms • 2–3 © 2009 Creative Teaching Press

Antonym Mini Book

Jake and Grandpa

_____
Name

1

Every summer Jake visits Grandpa. The two are very different. Jake is young and Grandpa is old.

_____

_____

2

Jake likes playing outdoors. Grandpa likes staying indoors.

_____

_____

3

Jake often keeps his bedroom messy. Grandpa always keeps his bedroom neat.

_____

_____

4

Jake often gets up late in the morning. Grandpa likes to get up early every day.

_____

_____

5

But Jake and Grandpa are alike in some ways. They both love each other a lot, and they hate to see the summer end!

_____

_____

6

Build-a-Skill Instant Books • Synonyms and Antonyms • 2–3 © 2009 Creative Teaching Press

Antonym Strip Book

Playtime Opposites

My yo-yo is **black**. Your yo-yo is _____.

My paint box is **heavy**. Your paint box is _____.

1

My toy plane flies **high**. Your toy plane flies _____.

My toy car is **speedy**. Your toy car is _____.

2

My stuffed bear is **large**. Your stuffed bear is _____.

My robot is **short**. Your robot is _____.

3

My doll can **giggle**. Your doll can _____.

My rubber duck gets **wet**. Your rubber duck

stays _____.

4

I like all my toys. You like your toys, too —

The ones that are **old** and the ones that are _____!

5

tall

cry

new

light

small

low

dry

white

slow

Build-a-Skill Instant Books • Synonyms and Antonyms • 2–3 © 2009 Creative Teaching Press

Antonym Mini Book

Sun's Up!

Name _____

1

Sun's up!
Are you awake?
Don't stay asleep,
For goodness sake!

_____

_____

2

Sun's up!
Let's go outside.
It's too nice
To stay inside!

_____

_____

3

Sun's up!
Let's climb a tree.
Up and down—
You and me!

_____

_____

4

Sun's up!
Let's ride our bikes.
Fast or slow—
Whatever you like!

_____

_____

5

Sun's up!
What a great day!
Before night comes,
Let's run and play!

_____

_____

6

Accordion-Fold Antonym Book

Everyday Opposites

Name _____

1

---

work   play

At school, I _____ hard in the classroom.

I _____ when I am at recess.

2

---

stop   go

On the street, I _____ when I am at a red light.

I _____ when the light turns green.

3

---

shout   whisper

At home, I _____ when I need to speak quietly.

I _____ when I need to call loudly.

4

---

cry   laugh

At the movies, I _____ when I see something sad.

I _____ when I see something funny.

5

---

give   receive

On my birthday, I _____ many gifts from family and friends.

Then I _____ everyone lots of hugs!

6

Build-a-Skill Instant Books • Synonyms and Antonyms • 2–3 © 2009 Creative Teaching Press

Nature Opposites

Name _____

1

slowly   swiftly

Snails move _____.

Cheetahs move _____.

2

sets   rises

The sun _____ in the morning.

The sun _____ in the evening.

3

above   below

Leaves grow _____ the ground.

Roots grow _____ the ground.

4

rough   smooth

Pebbles feel _____.

Tree bark feels _____.

5

daytime   nighttime

Bats hunt in the _____.

Eagles hunt in the _____.

6

Antonym Mini Book

Animal Look-Alikes

_____
Name

1

A frog and a toad look alike, but they are different.
A frog's skin is smooth while a toad's skin is bumpy.

_____

_____

2

A moth and a butterfly look alike, but they are different.
A moth's body is plump while a butterfly's body is slender.

_____

_____

3

A worm and a snake look alike, but they are different.
A worm's skin is moist while a snake's skin is dry.

_____

_____

4

A hare and a rabbit look alike, but they are different.
A hare is born furry while a rabbit is born hairless.

_____

_____

5

An alligator and a crocodile look alike, but they are different.
An alligator's snout is rounded while a crocodile's snout is pointed.

_____

_____

6

Build-a-Skill Instant Books • Synonyms and Antonyms • 2–3 © 2009 Creative Teaching Press